BARBARA JORDAN

BARBARA JORDAN

Voice of Democracy
by Lisa R. Rhodes

A Book Report Biography
FRANKLIN WATTS
A Division of Grolier Publishing
New York / London / Hong Kong / Sydney
Danbury, Connecticut

Cover illustration by Gary Overacre, interpreted from a photo by
Shelly Katz, Gamma Liaison

Photographs ©: AP/Wide World Photos: 98 (Taylor Johnson Pool), 2, 77;
Bill Malone: 67; Boston University Photo Services: 41; Martha Holmes: 86;
Texas Southern University: 102 (Moneta Sleet, Jr.), 24, 25, 31, 33, 35, 47,
62, 64, 100; UPI/Corbis-Bettmann: 8, 16, 49, 54, 58, 69, 73, 82, 84, 89, 92.

Visit Franklin Watts on the Internet at:
http://publishing.grolier.com

Library of Congress Cataloging-in-Publication Data

Rhodes, Lisa R.
Barbara Jordan : voice of democracy / by Lisa R. Rhodes.
    p. cm.— (A Book report biography)
Includes bibliographical references and index.
Summary: Traces the life and work of a pioneering African-American
woman who was a respected politician, teacher, and spokeswoman for
democracy.
ISBN 0-531-11450-3
1. Jordan, Barbara Charline, 1936–1996—Biography—Juvenile lit-
erature. 2. Women legislators—United States—Biography—Juvenile liter-
ature. 3. United States Congress—Biography—Juvenile literature. [1.
Jordan, Barbara Charline, 1936–1996 2. Women legislators] I. Title. II.
Series.
    E840.8J62R47 1998
    328.73'092—dc21   98-24134
                                                               CIP
                                                                AC

CONTENTS

CHAPTER ONE

A MATTER OF PRINCIPLE

President Richard Milhous Nixon pledged his innocence to the American public and refused to lift the veil of secrecy that protected his administration. It was early 1973, and rumors had spread through the nation's capital that several of the president's top aides were linked to a scandal called Watergate. Nixon, a member of the Republican Party, had just won his second presidential election in November 1972.

Five months earlier, on June 17, 1972, five men who worked for the president's reelection committee were arrested at 2:30 A.M. while breaking into the headquarters of the Democratic Party at the Watergate building in Washington, D.C. In the months after the arrest, Nixon and his administration managed to distance themselves from the break-in, clearing the way for a successful reelection campaign. By January 1973, however,

Throughout 1973 President Richard Nixon publicly denied any wrongdoing in the Watergate scandal.

suspicions began to grow that the break-in may have been part of a larger chain of illegal activities conducted by the Nixon administration.

Newspapers reported that the five men were looking for information about how much the Democrats knew about the Republican Party's campaign finances. However, President Nixon confidently told the nation he had no knowledge of the break-in.

A few months after the incident, the U.S. Senate voted to form a special committee to examine the rumors surrounding the scandal. Federal investigators found evidence that several top Nixon aides planned the break-in and later tried to cover up the incident after the men were arrested. Rumors spread that the president also helped to cover up the burglary.

As these events unfolded, Barbara Charline Jordan settled into her new role as a Democratic member of the U.S. House of Representatives. Back in November, at the same time Nixon was winning his reelection bid, Jordan had been elected to the House, making her the first black woman to represent a southern state in Congress. On the same day, Yvonne Braithwaite Burke, a Democrat from California, became the first black woman from that state to be elected to Congress. Both women joined Shirley Chisholm, the first black woman from any state to be elected to Congress, in the House of Representatives.

Jordan, who earned a law degree at Boston University, had served six years as a senator in the Texas state legislature. She represented black people and working class white people from Houston's Fifth Ward, one of the poorest sections in Texas and the neighborhood where she grew up.

INVESTIGATING THE SCANDAL

Soon after joining the House, Jordan was appointed to the House Judiciary Committee. This committee has many legal responsibilities. When the president is suspected of wrongdoing, this committee is responsible for recommending whether or not to charge the president with a crime. The process of charging the president with a crime is called impeachment.

. Jordan's character and political experience made her a well-qualified addition to the House Judiciary Committee. She hoped working for the committee would sharpen her legal skills and add prestige to her political career, but her experience on the committee surpassed all her expectations. Although it was in many ways a painful experience, Jordan's role on the committee would make her one of the most respected and trusted politicians in the country.

Jordan heard whispers about the president's involvement in Watergate, but she refused to believe them. In Texas, Jordan was known as a smart, straightforward, and hardworking public servant who knew how to cut a political deal without compromising her personal beliefs or making political enemies. She was the state's rising political star—a black woman and loyal Democrat who valued her supporters and the American legal system. Jordan respected the office of the president too much to accuse Nixon of wrongdoing without a lot of evidence to back up the charge.

President Nixon continued to deny all the rumors about Watergate and appointed Archibald Cox, a law professor at Harvard University, to be the special prosecutor in charge of the Watergate investigation. In July 1973, Cox asked the president to give investigators tape recordings he had made of meetings at the White House. The investigators hoped the tapes would reveal what, if anything, the president and his aides actually knew about the break-in. But the president refused to hand over the tapes.

In the fall of 1973, the House Judiciary Committee held hearings to approve Congressman Gerald Ford's nomination to the vice presidency. Spiro Agnew, Nixon's former vice president, had resigned after federal officials discovered he owed more than $200,000 in federal income taxes. President Nixon nominated Ford, a Republican from Michigan, to replace Agnew, but Jordan reviewed Ford's civil rights record and decided to vote against his nomination.

Despite Jordan's opposition, Congress approved Ford for the vice presidency. Soon after the approval hearings ended, the House Judiciary Committee turned its full attention to the Watergate scandal. President Nixon's refusal to cooperate with federal investigators worried Congress and the American public. The president ignored a federal court order to release the tapes and ordered the attorney general, the federal government's top legal officer, to fire Cox. The attorney general refused and resigned. The deputy attorney general, the second in command, also resigned rather than fire Cox. But the president was determined. He appointed Robert Bork, the solicitor general (a legal aide on the attorney general's staff), to the post of attorney general. Bork followed Nixon's request and fired Cox.

Cox's removal from the Watergate investigation forced Congress to take legal action against the president. The House of Representatives directed the Judiciary Committee to decide whether the evidence in the Watergate case supported any legal grounds for impeaching the president. If the committee recommended impeachment, the issue would be put to a vote in the House of Representatives. Two-thirds of the members of the House had to vote in favor of impeachment in order to charge the president with a crime. If impeached, the Senate would conduct a trial to determine if the president was guilty of the charges brought against him. If convicted at the trial, the president would be removed from office.

No American president had ever been impeached. Jordan carefully studied the U.S. Constitution and many legal writings about the impeachment process. The committee was given an awesome responsibility, and Jordan wanted to be absolutely certain her discussion in the matter was based on legal facts. "I was not going to vote to impeach Richard Nixon because I didn't like him," Jordan wrote in *Barbara Jordan: A Self-Portrait*, her autobiography. She

"I was not going to vote to impeach Richard Nixon because I didn't like him."

hoped the committee would find grounds to clear the president and his administration of wrong-doing. She knew a presidential impeachment could ruin the public's trust in the federal government.

Many Americans were already skeptical of the federal government. The Vietnam War, a military conflict thousands of miles away, had divided the country. Young American soldiers had been helping the South Vietnamese government fight Communist rebels in North Vietnam since the late 1950s. Some Americans believed the war was taking the lives of far too many young soldiers and that the government was spending too many tax dollars interfering in the affairs of two

foreign countries. Other Americans believed it was the government's duty to help defeat the North Vietnamese to prevent the spread of Communism, a form of government that rivaled American democracy.

President Lyndon B. Johnson, Nixon's predecessor, had refused to run for the presidency for a second term because he could not end the war in a peaceful manner without damaging the country's reputation as a defender of democracy. In 1973, the Nixon administration began negotiations with South and North Vietnam to end the war and bring American troops home. However, the loss of American lives had touched the nation deeply. Some Americans doubted the federal government's efforts and remained skeptical. Congress also refused to approve the president's request for money to bomb Cambodia, a country many American military officials believed supplied military aid to the North Vietnamese. The president's efforts abroad did little to improve his public image at home.

In April 1974, the Nixon administration released an edited transcript of several White House tapes, but the gesture did little to convince investigators that the president intended to cooperate with federal authorities. The mounting evidence in the Watergate case could not be ignored.

By mid-July, the Judiciary Committee was ready to present the results of its research and vote on the possibility of impeachment. Each committee member prepared a 15-minute speech on whether or not to recommend impeachment of the president. All of the speeches would be televised.

WE THE PEOPLE

On the first day of committee speeches, Jordan was still outlining her legal argument for impeachment of the president. After weeks of study, Jordan had become convinced that the evidence showed the president knew about the break-in before it happened and that his conduct after the incident was illegal. To support her opinion, Jordan relied heavily on the Constitution. Her belief in the document's principles about liberty and justice was unshakable.

On July 25, 1974, Jordan sat in her committee-chamber seat and told the entire nation why she would vote to impeach Richard Nixon, the 37th president of the United States. Jordan held eight pages of notes about impeachment in her hand. She looked directly into the television camera and read the Preamble of the Constitution. Her own speech was still unwritten. Her thoughts came as she spoke.

As a member of the House Judiciary Committee, Jordan delivers her speech recommending the impeachment of President Nixon.

'We the people'—it is a very eloquent beginning. But when the Constitution of the United States was completed on the 17th of September in 1787, I was not included in that 'We the people.' I felt for many years that somehow George Washington and

Alexander Hamilton just left me out by mistake. But through the process of amendment, interpretation, and court decision, I have finally been included in 'We the people.'

Today I am an inquisitor. I believe hyperbole would not be fictional and would not overstate the solemnness that I feel right now. My faith in the Constitution is whole. It is complete. It is total. I am not going to sit here and be an idle spectator to the diminution, the subversion, the destruction of the Constitution.

During her speech, Jordan frequently referred to the words of the founders of the United States:

James Madison said in the Virginia Ratification Convention: 'If the President be connected in any suspicious manner with any person and there be grounds to believe that he will shelter him, he may be impeached.'

We have heard time and time again that the evidence reflects payment to the defendants of money. The President has knowledge that these funds were being paid and that these funds were collected for the 1972 presidential campaign.

We know that the President met with Mr. Henry Petersen [the assistant attorney general] 27 times to discuss matters related to Watergate, and immediately thereafter met with the very persons who were implicated in the information Mr. Petersen was receiving and transmitting to the President.

Jordan concluded her address with these words:

If the impeachment provision in the Constitution of the United States will not reach the offenses charged here, then perhaps that 18th century Constitution should be abandoned to a 20th century paper shredder. Has the President committed offenses and planned and directed and acquiesced in a course of conduct which the Constitution will not tolerate? That is the question. . . . We should now forthwith proceed to answer the question. It is reason and not passion which must guide out deliberations, guide our debate, and guide our decision.

Jordan placed her vote for impeachment and left the chamber with several other committee members. "I didn't like the idea of working to impeach the President. . . . I wished that it had not been necessary to do that. I really did," Jordan said years later in her autobiography. After her moving speech, Jordan cried alone in an empty room.

The Judiciary Committee found that the president had obstructed justice on three major counts. The committee recommended that the president be impeached on the grounds that he helped to cover up the Watergate break-in, abused his presidential powers (by misusing government agencies such as the FBI and IRS), and disobeyed legal orders to release evidence to federal investigators.

The House of Representatives was expected to vote overwhelmingly in favor of the committee's impeachment recommendation, but the president removed himself from office before the House had an opportunity to vote. President Nixon resigned from office on August 9, 1974, and later received a federal pardon.

Jordan, however, earned the respect and trust of millions of Americans after her televised speech. She received countless letters of thanks and admiration from people all over the country. Jordan received praise for her "eloquence, forthrightness, incisive rationality, and dignity." Some called her speech a "literary masterpiece." Some listeners were moved to tears. "You have changed the minds of myself, my wife, our relatives, and all our friends," one man wrote. "We thought only a man should be president, but all of us will vote for you, any black man or lady."

No other black politician, male or female, had ever spoken to a national audience about a legal subject as important as the impeachment of an American president. Jordan's tall stature, confident speaking voice, high intellect, broad smile, and easygoing manner shattered negative stereotypes about black Americans, whom the media often portrayed as uneducated and lazy. Few other black leaders have had the opportunity to profoundly influence the way American society views its black citizens.

Throughout her congressional career, Jordan continued to probe the nation's conscience. Jordan's work during the Watergate hearings remained one of her most noteworthy accomplishments, but she also worked diligently to pass important laws demanding equal rights for all people. She became an influential member of the Democratic Party, an advocate for liberal causes, and a popular law professor. In the years before her death, Jordan spoke out against the nomination of Robert Bork, the former political ally of President Nixon, to serve on the Supreme Court. She also led a federal commission to improve the nation's immigration laws.

"There is no black woman in politics today that is not in her [Jordan's] debt."

"There is no black woman in politics today that is not in her [Jordan's] debt," said Eleanor Holmes Norton, a black woman and the congressional delegate for the District of Columbia, in a 1996 *Washington Post* article. "She taught us how to take charge."

Jordan overcame racism, sexism, and a crippling physical disability to craft a political career few other American leaders can match. "I am neither a black politician, nor a female politician, [I am] just a politician," Jordan once said, recalling her career.

In truth, Barbara Charline Jordan was much more. Her life began in a small southern town, miles away from the power and intrigue she later found in Washington, D.C.

CHAPTER TWO

HOME

No one was happier than John Ed Patten when his youngest granddaughter, Barbara Charline Jordan, came into the world on February 21, 1936, in Houston, Texas. Born to Patten's oldest daughter, Arlyne, young Barbara was so beloved by her grandfather that he carried a picture of her everywhere. Patten wrote the phrase "My Heart" on the back of Barbara's picture to show everyone that his granddaughter was the love of his life.

John Ed Patten treasured the dark-skinned, bright-eyed newborn, but it was Charles Jordan, Barbara's paternal grandfather, who helped provide a roof over her head. For the first 12 years of her life, Barbara and her family lived with Grandfather Jordan in a two-bedroom brick house trimmed with pink paint. The Jordans lived in an all-black neighborhood in Houston's Fifth Ward, one of the poorest areas in Texas. Benjamin Jordan, Barbara's father, had bought the house with Charles, his father, years earlier and made it the Jordan family's home.

Benjamin Jordan and Arlyne Patten Jordan were hardworking parents determined to mold their three daughters—Rose Mary, the oldest, Bennie, and Barbara—into well-educated Christian women. Benjamin worked at the Houston Terminal Warehouse and Cold Storage Company and ruled his home with a stern hand. As Barbara grew older, Benjamin would not allow his daughters to smoke, drink, play cards, or attend movies. Dancing was also out of the question. Instead, he kept his daughters busy with school work, church, and piano lessons.

Benjamin wanted the best for his daughters and expected nothing less from them. He attended Tuskegee Institute (an all-black college in Alabama founded by black leader Booker T. Washington in 1881) but did not graduate. Benjamin's mother became ill, and he was forced to drop out of school because his family could no longer afford to pay for his education. Benjamin returned to Houston and landed a warehouse job. He joined the choir at Good Hope Missionary Baptist Church and met his future wife, young Arlyne Patten.

Arlyne, a high-school graduate, worked cleaning the homes of white families to make ends

*Young Barbara stands between her sisters
Bennie (left) and Rose Mary.*

meet. The congregation at Good Hope admired
her fine public-speaking skills, and many members of the church insisted Arlyne would make a
mighty powerful preacher if she were a man. But
when Arlyne captured Benjamin's heart, plans for

marriage and children replaced her dreams of becoming a secretary. Her father, John Ed Patten, was disappointed that Arlyne gave up her occupational dreams for domestic responsibilities. He had hoped Arlyne would go on to college and

John Ed Patten

refine her speaking skills. Instead, Arlyne and her new husband moved in with Grandfather Jordan and filled their home with gospel music.

Early in her life, Barbara spent much time in church. Every Sunday, the Jordans worshiped at Good Hope along with other black families. Grandfather Jordan was chairman of the deacon board, and Benjamin continued to sing in the choir. Barbara sang too, along with her sisters. The girls eventually formed a trio called the Jordan sisters. Miss Mattie Thomas, a music teacher who organized recitals at the church, taught the Jordan girls piano and insisted that they practice every day. Barbara studied for two years but later gave up her lessons to ride a bicycle. She continued singing with her sisters and learned to appreciate music for the rest of her life.

GRANDFATHER PATTEN

The Jordans ate dinner with Grandfather Patten every Sunday after services. Patten himself did not attend church, though he read the Bible regularly. He developed his own brand of Christianity and lived by his own moral code. Patten was one of the few people young Barbara knew who had suffered the injustices of racism first hand. In 1918, Patten was married with three children and owned a restaurant and candy store. One evening,

Patten was arrested by police when they claimed he tried to shoot and kill another white police officer during a burglary at his store. An all-white jury convicted Patten, and he was sentenced to ten years in jail, despite the testimony of a doctor who told the court that Patten was shot in the hand while trying to surrender to police.

It was not uncommon for black people in the South to find injustice in a court of law. The southern United States was a place where black and white Americans lived separately—and unequally. Black people were victims of racial prejudice, and the nation's laws allowed black people to be treated like second-class citizens—even after slavery officially came to an end in 1863. Laws throughout the south prevented black Americans from attending the same public schools, eating in the same restaurants, or using the same public bathrooms as white people. Black people were discriminated against in the workplace and often subjected to racial slurs. Black and white people also lived in separate neighborhoods.

When Barbara was a young girl, she had few public black American role models to look up to. Barbara and her sisters went to school with other black children and rarely saw white people in their neighborhood. The life of white Americans was a mystery—and Barbara's family did their best to protect her from the cruelties of racism.

Grandfather Patten did his best to prepare Barbara for the unkind world that waited for her as an adult. Every Sunday afternoon, he and Barbara spent time together after dinner while Rose Mary and Bennie went back to church for more Bible lessons. Patten taught Barbara how to think for herself and stand on her own two feet. Barbara helped her grandfather collect and sell pieces of old steel and iron for his junkyard, and he paid her an allowance for her work. In the evening, he read verses from the Bible and taught Barbara his own interpretation of Christian living. "Don't get sidetracked and be like everybody else. Do what you're going to do on the basis of your own ingenuity," Patten told his granddaughter. "[You can't] trust the world out there. [You can't] trust them, so you [have] to figure things out for yourself. But you [have] to love humanity."

> **"Don't get sidetracked and be like everybody else. Do what you're going to do on the basis of your own ingenuity."**

When Barbara was 10, she decided it was time to be baptized. She had promised Grandfather Patten that she would follow the example of Jesus Christ and become a Christian disciple when she was 12, but she changed her mind. Benjamin Jordan was happy and proud when his daughter decided to become a member of Good Hope. Two years later, Benjamin received God's calling and became a minister of his own church called the Greater Pleasant Hill Baptist Church. At this church, Barbara discovered that she, like her mother, had a talent for public speaking. To help raise money for her father's ministry, Barbara began reciting speeches and poems. Her favorite and most requested poem was "The Creation: A Negro Sermon," by James Weldon Johnson, a black poet.

A STRONG WILL

By the time she entered Phyllis Wheatley High School (an all-black school named after another famous black poet), Barbara was ready to test her father's patience. Although Benjamin approved of Barbara's religious conversion, he was displeased to find that his youngest daughter could be quite stubborn and defiant. Benjamin insisted that his family eat very little meat, but Barbara loved it. Grandfather Patten and Barbara ate barbecue ribs every Sunday evening, and she felt she should be able to eat meat at dinner time during the week. When Benjamin told Barbara to buy her own meat and eat it, she did—thanks to her allowance from Grandfather Patten. But she refused to share her food with her sisters. On another occasion, Benjamin refused to buy his daughter an expensive winter coat. Barbara saved her money and bought it herself. When Benjamin bragged about the new coat to a friend, Barbara proudly boasted that her father did not buy it. Benjamin was shocked that his daughter dared to mock him in public. Despite his attempts to keep a tight reign on his daughters, Benjamin could not keep hold of Barbara's strong will.

Barbara was a good student in school. She tutored classmates in geometry and chemistry. But during her first two years of high school, having fun and making new friends was the top priority. By her early teens, Barbara had shed her tomboy image, and riding a bicycle was out of the question. The teenage Barbara wore dresses, walked in toeless shoes, and styled her hair in a pageboy. She took a driver's education course and at age 14 began to drive her father's car to take friends to the local soda-pop store after school. The Jordan family now lived in a new house not far from Grandfather Jordan. The black neighborhood was quiet, and adults worked at local schools or stores. Barbara and her sister Bennie made friends with Evelyn and Mary Elizabeth Justice, two neighborhood girls, and walked to Phyllis Wheatley every day.

Barbara was tall and full-figured, but she didn't play any high school sports. She joined sev-

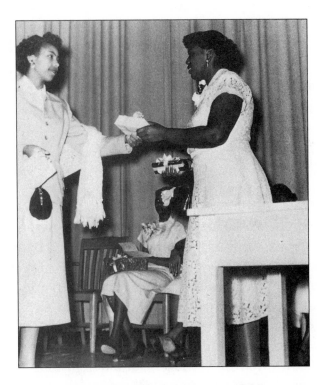

As a high school senior in 1952,
Barbara is named Girl of the Year.

eral school clubs instead and cheered for her home
team at football games. She sang with her sister
in the all-girl choir at school and convinced her
mother to allow her to throw slumber parties at
home.

Barbara was elected president of her school's
honor society in her sophomore year, and teachers

began to notice her gift for public speaking. Barbara loved reciting poems and speeches. The years of practice in church gave Barbara all the confidence she needed. Ashton Jerome Oliver, the high school oratory coach, asked Barbara to join the debate team. She was anxious to take on a new challenge.

SUCCESS ON THE DEBATE TEAM

The high school debate team became a regular winner at local, regional, and district competitions against other black schools. Barbara brought home medals all the time, to the delight of her mother, Arlyne. In 1952, Barbara won first place in a state oratory contest in Waco, Texas. Winning had become so easy, Barbara had forgotten what it felt like to lose. But a defeat in an Elks Oratorical Contest gave Barbara a jolt. Her persuasive and forthright style earned her favor with the judges, but her male competitors were more emotional, like the ministers Barbara heard on Sundays in church. Barbara placed as a runner-up in the Elks competition, but the win in Waco had made her the state favorite in an upcoming National Ushers Convention Oratorical Contest in Chicago. Barbara decided to brush up on her theatrical skills and put a little zest into her presentation to win in Chicago.

Barbara's instincts were right. Her speech earned her first place, a $200 scholarship to the college of her choice, and a literary medal. On July 27, 1952, the *Houston Informer*, the local newspaper, published an article about Barbara's win and quoted her thoughts

"It's just another milestone I passed. It's just the beginning."

Barbara (second from left) wins first prize at the National Ushers Convention Oratorical Contest in Chicago in 1952.

about the event. "It's just another milestone I passed," young Barbara told the newspaper. "It's just the beginning."

During her last two years at Phyllis Wheatley, Barbara began to think about her plans for college. Barbara knew that she wanted to live a life that was different than the one she knew in Houston. Legal segregation—the separation of the races—and racial discrimination were facts of life that Barbara despised, but she saw nothing she could do to change things. "I decided that if I was going to be outstanding or different, it was going to be in relation to other black people, rather than getting somewhere where white people were," Barbara wrote years later in her autobiography. "It seemed an impossibility to make any transition to the larger world out there."

But Barbara's views changed when Edith Sampson, a highly respected black lawyer from Chicago, visited Phyllis Wheatley on a special career day. Barbara had never met a black lawyer, and she was impressed. Sampson's success in a legal career—particularly as a woman—inspired Barbara to become a lawyer.

COLLEGE BOUND

Barbara enrolled at Texas Southern University (TSU), an all-black college in Houston, in 1952.

*Barbara (second from left) as junior class vice
president in 1955 at Texas Southern University*

She signed up for liberal arts courses, pledged
Delta Sigma Theta, a black women's sorority, and
joined the debate team. The debate team traveled
around the country competing against other black
colleges—and white universities. Barbara contin-

ued to beat her competitors and sharpen her skills, but she didn't debate white students until her junior year in 1954. Dr. Tom Freeman, the team's debate coach, entered Barbara in a debate contest at Baylor University in Waco, Texas. Barbara won first prize against a team of white young ladies. The experience was one that Barbara treasured because it gave her a chance to compete on the same level with students from different backgrounds and races—a rare opportunity in the South. The victory made the impossible seem possible—perhaps black people and white people could relate to each other as equals.

The debate team at Harvard University competed against TSU the following year. The outcome of the contest—a tie—boosted Barbara's confidence. Barbara wanted to become a lawyer—why not apply to Harvard Law School?

As Barbara considered applying to the predominantly white institution, the United States Supreme Court was taking steps to integrate all of America's

"We conclude that in the field of public education, the doctrine of 'separate but equal' has no place. Separate educational facilities are inherently unequal."

—Supreme Court, May 17, 1954

schools. On May 17, 1954, the Court, in a case called *Brown v. Board of Education*, declared that the legal separation of black and white children in public schools was unconstitutional. "We conclude that in the field of public education, the doctrine of 'separate but equal' has no place. Separate educational facilities are inherently unequal." The Court's decision paved the way for the end of legal segregation by requiring public schools to open their doors to black people with "all deliberate speed."

The Supreme Court decision was an important victory for the entire black community. The National Association for the Advancement of Colored People (NAACP), the oldest civil-rights organization in the country, argued the case in front of the Supreme Court on behalf of black America. The NAACP's lawyers hoped the Court would end centuries of legal racial discrimination against black people, making it possible for black children to take advantage of opportunities that were denied their parents and grandparents. The Court's ruling meant the nation could no longer deny or ignore unjust laws that denied citizens their basic rights because of their race. The Jordans and other black families hoped the Supreme Court's decision would bring positive social change.

Barbara hoped to bring about social change herself, and Harvard seemed like the perfect place to begin. But Dr. Freeman advised Barbara to apply to Boston University's law school instead. He reasoned that Barbara, as a student from a public university, would have a better chance of getting into Boston University (BU). Barbara heeded his advice and applied to Boston University.

By this time, Rose Mary had already graduated from Prairie View College, and Bennie had graduated from TSU. Benjamin and Arlyne managed their finances so all three of their daughters could finish college, but paying for Boston University was going to be quite a stretch. However, the family decided Barbara could attend Boston University no matter the cost—if she was accepted.

Barbara graduated with honors from TSU in 1956 with a degree in political science and history. She also received an acceptance notice from Boston University. Barbara packed her bags and wrapped her family's hopes and dreams around her heart. She wasn't sure what life would hold beyond the protective boundaries of her neighborhood, but Barbara Jordan was growing up. It was time to leave home.

CHAPTER THREE

A LADY OF POLITICS

The Boston University School of Law was a long way from the close-knit black community that nurtured Jordan's self-esteem and her dreams to become a lawyer.

Jordan wasn't quite sure what to expect when she arrived on campus in the fall of 1956. The three-day car ride from Houston showed Jordan many aspects of American society. The beginning of the trip took her past the crop fields and rickety wooden homes of poor black field and factory workers. She rode past clusters of small, segregated white towns in the South. Her trip ended among the clean-paved streets, stately homes, and well-kept lawns of Boston's affluent, predominantly white neighborhoods. In this strange new world, black students—and women of any color— were rare additions to a law classroom, and influential families often pulled strings to land their sons jobs at prominent law firms after graduation.

Jordan relied on a $20-a-month allowance, sent from Rose Mary and Bennie, who were now teachers in Houston, to meet her daily needs. Jordan knew no one in the city to help her find part-time or summer work or a first job after she graduated. She was one of six women (and one of two black women) in a freshman class of 600 law students. Her only advantages were her determination and considerable intellect.

The first year of law school was rough. Jordan found every class difficult, the legal language and theories complicated and lengthy. After a few weeks, Jordan knew that completing the law program would require many hours of consistent study. Every evening after class, Jordan took her law books to the graduate dorm library and read chapter after chapter until the early hours of the morning. She averaged only three to four hours of sleep a night, but without the additional study time, Jordan believed she would fall behind her classmates. Jordan knew she had the ability to do well, but she also recognized that even the best education at an all-black college did not prepare her for the rigors of a predominantly white institution such as Boston University.

"I realized that the best training available in an all-black university was not equal to the best training one developed as a white university student. Separate was not equal; it just wasn't," Jordan wrote in her auto-biography. Despite the fact that Jordan graduated with honors from TSU, racial segregation made it

"Separate was not equal; it just wasn't."

*Jordan as a law student at
Boston University*

difficult for her and other black students to receive the same quality of education as white students.

Understanding her coursework was a constant struggle, but by the time she took her midterm exam in criminal law, Jordan was almost sure she would earn a passing grade. The half-year course seemed a bit less difficult than the other law courses because Jordan was familiar with the language in the criminal-law textbooks. On the day of the mid-term exam, however, Jordan couldn't believe her eyes. The exam questions were far more complicated than she had anticipated—the answers were not simply a matter of "guilty" or "not guilty." Students had to explain—in detail—what legal cases supported their point of view and what legal logic made their answers correct. "What I couldn't focus on during the exam was that it was not the answer the professor was trying to pull from me. It was the reasoning," Jordan recalled. She tried her best, but Jordan thought she had failed the exam.

After class, there was nothing she could do but watch a film at a local movie theater to escape into a world of fantasy. "I sat there

"I sat there for three hours wondering how I was going to lay it on my father that I had just busted out of law school."

for three hours wondering how I was going to lay it on my father that I had just busted out of law school," Jordan said. She assumed that her education at Boston University was over.

Jordan was wrong. She earned a 79 on the exam—a passing grade—and gained the confidence to stay in school. In addition to the long hours in the library, Jordan joined a study group of other black students in the spring. The study group gave Jordan the chance to discuss and debate legal facts with her peers. Slowly, she began to feel at ease with the process of legal thinking. By the end of her first year, Jordan had earned a B average and the self-assurance to complete law school. "If I can survive the first year," Jordan said, "I'll make it the rest of the way."

Jordan devoted most of her second semester at BU to study. However, she also began to relax and find suitable social activities on campus, including a few small parties with friends. Jordan continued to practice her religious faith while in law school. Every Sunday, Jordan attended the university's Marsh Chapel and listened to Howard Thurman, a black minister and dean of the chapel, preach the Christian gospel.

Jordan enjoyed Thurman's sermons and began to view religion and God differently than she had as a child. In her autobiography, Jordan wrote that she no longer feared punishment for sin, but instead learned about God's love and forgiveness. She found comfort in this new religious interpretation and was so moved by Thurman that she thought about dropping out of law school to pursue a degree in theology. But after some deep thought, Jordan decided against the pastoral path and reasoned that God really wanted her to become a lawyer.

Jordan's renewed spiritual faith helped her to feel more secure in her new environment, and it showed in her studies. During her second year in law school, a law professor suggested that Jordan apply for a summer job at the law office of Edward Brooke, a black lawyer in Boston. Jordan followed the professor's advice. Unfortunately, she didn't land a job, but she was glad to know her hard work was paying off—and that a BU professor recognized her potential. Later, in 1966, Brooke became the first black man to represent Massachusetts in the U.S. Senate. He served until 1978.

In June 1959, Jordan received her law degree after three years of consistent study. Jordan felt it wouldn't be fair to ask her parents and sisters to take on the additional expense of traveling to Boston, so she asked her family not to come to the graduation ceremony. But nothing could keep her family away on such a special day. Jordan's father bought a new car and drove the entire family to see his daughter graduate from one of the best law schools in the country.

Unfortunately, the one person closest to Jordan's heart was absent on her graduation day. Grandfather Patten had died several years earlier from an injury he received in a railroad train accident. Jordan skipped several law classes at the time of the accident and rushed home to see her beloved grandfather in the hospital. But there was little chance for his recovery. Patten died soon after, leaving Jordan memories of his courage, strength, and love.

OUT IN THE WORLD

Jordan's law school graduation marked the end of a period of self-doubt and fear of failure. Now a young woman, Jordan was ready for her future. Jordan hoped to start her law career in Massachusetts. She had lived in the integrated North for three years, and it seemed that the job prospects for a young, educated black woman would be more plentiful than in the South, where racial segregation was slowly becoming an evil memory. Jordan took the Massachusetts bar exam to earn a license to practice law in the state. She also went on a few job interviews, but with no success. Jordan didn't have the connections to the legal field that many other BU law graduates enjoyed. Without these connections, a promising job was hard to find. After an unsuccessful summer, Jordan returned to Texas and moved in with her family. She passed the state's bar exam, earned her license, and began to serve clients from her home town.

The first few months were slow. Jordan's light client load left her with a few extra hours to spare, so she decided to volunteer at the Harris County Democratic Headquarters. The 1960 presidential campaign for John F. Kennedy, a Democrat from Massachusetts, and vice presidential candidate Lyndon B. Johnson, a Democrat from Texas, was well underway. Jordan volunteered for a blockworker program designed to get out the vote in forty black voting precincts in the county. Jordan helped coordinate mass mailings and other administrative duties, and eventually she began making speeches at black churches and political, civic, and social groups on behalf of Harris County Democrats. Jordan's legal training and her years as a champion debater equipped her with the skills to make moving speeches. She enjoyed traveling from town to town in her new car (which she purchased after starting her law practice), encouraging black people to cast their vote for Democratic candidates.

When the presidential campaign ended in the fall of 1960, Jordan decided to continue her volunteer work. She received a warm response from the local black community, and it was no surprise. Black people throughout the South were deter-

Jordan as a young attorney in the early 1960s

mined to exercise their political power. Tens of thousands of southern black people took part in a grassroots protest called the Civil Rights movement. In communities across the South, black people participated in nonviolent marches, economic boycotts, and voter registration drives to demand an end to racial injustice and segregation.

Dr. Martin Luther King Jr., a black Baptist minister from Atlanta, Georgia, was one of the most prominent leaders of the movement. Dr. King headed an organization called the Southern Christian Leadership Conference (SCLC), dedicated to ensuring civil rights for black Americans. Dr. King and the SCLC challenged the nation's city, state, and national political leaders to strike down racial segregation laws. Dr. King hoped the Civil Rights movement would guarantee black Americans the same rights and privileges white Americans enjoyed—the right to a job that provides enough money to support one's family, get a quality education, live in a safe neighborhood, vote for a political candidate, receive a fair hearing in a court of law, and gain access to affordable health care and other important social services. Jordan's speeches echoed Dr. King's call for racial equality at the ballot box. Black people in areas such as Houston's Fifth Ward eagerly supported the struggle for civil rights.

In the spring of 1961, Jordan decided to take a break from her legal work and political speech-

Dr. Martin Luther King Jr. speaks during
a civil rights march in Washington, D.C.,
on August 28, 1963.

es to teach a course on politics and government.
She applied to six colleges for a summer teaching
position and landed a job at Tuskegee Institute,
the college her father had attended in Alabama.
When Jordan returned to Texas in the fall, she
used the extra money to open a law office in down-

town Houston. Jordan shared the office with a high school friend who had also become a lawyer.

RUNNING FOR OFFICE

The new law office gave Jordan a feeling of professional security, and her interest in politics began to grow. The Civil Rights movement forced political leaders and local citizens to move toward integration and racial equality. Jordan was "bitten by the political bug." Her legal background gave her the intellectual foundation she needed for a career in politics. "My interest [in politics] which had been latent was sparked," Jordan wrote in her autobiography.

> **"My interest [in politics] which had been latent was sparked."**

Jordan borrowed $500 from a friend and paid the fee to become a candidate in the 1962 election for a senate seat in the Texas House of Representatives. Twelve candidates campaigned for the Democratic seat. Jordan was the only black person and the only female Democratic candidate. Jordan traveled across Harris County giving speeches about liberal causes, such as state finances, welfare, and education. She also read everything she could find about the Texas state government.

Jordan received standing ovations and cheers from voters during her speeches. But on election day, she lost. Jordan garnered only 46,000 votes, while her opponent, Willis Whitley, a conservative white lawyer, pulled in 65,000. Jordan received the majority of black votes, but the white liberals who cheered at her speeches gave their votes to other candidates.

The election results puzzled Jordan. Her political friends in Harris County believed the loss was part of being a new face in Texas politics. But an educator at a prominent university thought differently. He told Jordan that her image—black, female, and full-figured—was not appealing to voters. He suggested that it would be tough for Jordan to get elected to the Texas state legislature. Jordan didn't agree with his point of view. She believed the people of Texas were smart and fair. A competent black woman, no matter what her dress size, could surely win a Texas state election. Jordan was determined to prove it.

Jordan ran for the senate seat again in 1964—and lost. This time, Jordan realized that her race, and perhaps her marital status, might be political obstacles. Jordan was a black candidate in a county where votes in black districts were not equal to votes in white districts. No matter how many black people voted for Jordan, she could never win against a white candidate. The fact that Jordan was still single did not help her case. She wore soft colors and flattering dresses throughout the second campaign in an attempt to change her public image, but Southern voters, regardless of race, respected traditional family values. Jordan did not represent the traditional role of wife and mother.

Losing two political campaigns was a tough blow for Jordan. But she was not willing to compromise her convictions. Jordan knew she wanted a life in politics, and she believed her race and gender should not matter. For the meantime, however, Jordan decided to put her political future on hold and devote her time to her legal career. She worked at her law office and took a part-time job as an administrative assistant for a county judge. Jordan could not change the political climate in Texas. Texas had to change for her.

Texas did change. But it took several Supreme Court rulings to create the political environment that allowed Jordan to launch her career as an elected official. States in the South often created voting districts that intentionally divided black communities among several different districts. This ensured that black voters remained a small minority in each district, and it gave white political candidates an advantage over their black counterparts. In 1964, the Supreme Court required states to redraw the boundary lines of voting districts so that no group of people would be given an unfair advantage.

In 1965, Harris County followed the Court's orders and created a new 11th State Senatorial District. The new voting district included Jordan's Fifth Ward. Thirty-eight percent of the ward's voters were black, and a large number of voters were working-class white people and Latinos. These voters had supported Jordan during her previous two campaigns.

Jordan declared her third candidacy for the Texas state senate in February 1966. This time, she was prepared to win. Jordan's opponent, Charles Whitfield, was a seasoned white liberal politician with strong ties to the working class. Whitfield had won every race in his political career.

Jordan set up her campaign headquarters one block away from her law office in the Fifth Ward. She quit her job with the county judge and used her savings to hire a personal secretary and a campaign manager. The Jordan political team mailed out sample voting ballots to 35,000 black voters in the new district.

In March, Jordan won the endorsement of the Harris County Executive Committee. But Whitfield decided to fight back hard. His campaign literature attacked what he called the 11th District's "Black Block Vote" and urged voters to reconsider his years of political experience. Whitfield claimed

*Jordan shows the victory sign after
being elected to the Texas State Senate on
May 8, 1966.*

that a 30-year-old black woman could not represent the district's interests.

But the voters disagreed with Whitfield. On
May 8, 1966, Jordan beat her opponent two votes
to one and became the first black woman to win a

seat in the Texas State Senate. Fifty-two percent of 11th District voters were black, but Jordan won 68 percent of the total district vote—including 30 to 50 percent of the vote in white areas. Jordan, the hometown girl from the Fifth Ward, finally made good. White liberal politicians throughout Harris County did not forget her loyalty to the Democratic party. The years Jordan spent encouraging black Democrats to vote, and her determination to run for office three times, impressed her political allies. Despite her lack of political experience, Jordan had earned her own brand of political clout. The door to Texas politics was now wide open.

CHAPTER FOUR

CONGRESSWOMAN JORDAN

Lyndon B. Johnson was a farm boy from Texas who learned how to play the shrewd game of politics during more than 10 years of service in the U.S. House of Representatives and the U.S. Senate. In 1960, he was elected vice president under President John F. Kennedy, a fellow Democrat. Three years later, Johnson was quickly sworn in as president when Kennedy was assassinated during a trip to Dallas, Texas.

Johnson, also known as "LBJ," now led the country during the turbulent struggle for civil rights. Kennedy died before he could approve legislation that would guarantee equal rights for black people and citizens of all races. But Johnson, a tough politician and warm-hearted southerner, was determined to press on with the effort to guarantee equal rights. He worked with Congress to pass civil rights laws and other legislation to improve the lives of the poor. Johnson called his campaign for social progress the "Great Society."

Many members of Congress, particularly those from the South, were not anxious to support civil rights laws. The prospect of full racial equality threatened some traditions of southern life. The Civil Rights movement and the progress of legal battles for integration in southern courts pushed politicians and the entire nation to confront America's history of racial intolerance.

By the time Jordan was elected to the Texas State Senate, President Johnson had signed two major civil rights laws and made his Great Society campaign a top priority. The Civil Rights Act of 1964, the strongest civil rights law in the country, forbids discrimination based on color, race, national origin, religion, and sex. The Civil Rights Act of 1965 eliminated the use of reading and writing tests to determine who is qualified to vote. Before this law was passed, poor, uneducated black people in the South were required to pass reading and writing tests in order to register to vote. However, white people were not required to do so—even, in some cases, when they were known to be illiterate.

Jordan, and other black leaders throughout the nation, supported the president's agenda. She worked tirelessly on several political committees in the senate and studied important policies and procedures. Jordan had become the first black

*President Lyndon B. Johnson shakes hands with
Dr. Martin Luther King Jr. after signing the
Civil Rights Act of 1964.*

woman to serve in the Texas legislature at a very
critical time in the nation's history—and she was
determined to succeed. The white men who
worked with Jordan were not sure whether to wel-
come her to the "good ol' boys" club of Texas politics, but their response to her race and gender did

not shake her confidence. Jordan took care not to emphasize her race or gender with her colleagues. Instead she focused on her work and used her straightforward style and sense of fair play to build political alliances that would help her represent the 11th District.

RISING STAR

President Johnson invited Jordan and several other influential black leaders to attend a special White House meeting in 1967. The president hoped to pass a fair housing law, but he wanted to discuss the matter with national leaders who represented the poor. The invitation surprised Jordan, but her reputation had convinced the president that she was a political ally who could not be overlooked. Jordan flew to Washington, D.C., on February 13 and joined three civil rights activists—Roy Wilkins, Whitney Young, and Dorothy Height—in a private meeting with the president. Jordan listened to the details of the housing proposal and encouraged the president to write a comprehensive housing law. President Johnson and several news reporters were impressed with Jordan's knowledge of the housing discrimination issue. Jordan's trip made newspaper headlines the next day.

Jordan returned to Texas and turned her attention to a bill that proposed to increase taxes for the state's poorest citizens. She quickly wrote a speech calling for the bill's defeat since poor families already paid 30 percent of their wages in taxes. The other state senators cheered Jordan's speech and later voted against the bill. Jordan did not intend to forget the poor and working-class voters who elected her to office.

As a member of the Labor and Management Legislation Committee, Jordan presented her first bill to the state legislature a short time later. She wrote the state's Fair Employment Practices Act to forbid discrimination in hiring employees. The bill passed 30 votes to 1. Before the end of her first term, Jordan also helped defeat a controversial spending bill proposed by Texas governor John Connally.

The senate named Jordan "Outstanding Freshman Senator" to reward her for her legislative efforts during her first term. Jordan, deeply touched by the honor, gave a personal speech on the senate floor. "When I first got here we approached each other with suspicion, fear, and apprehension," Jordan said. "But now I can call each of you, singularly, friend."

> **"When I first got here we approached each other with suspicion, fear, and apprehension. But now I can call each of you, singularly, friend."**

The voters of the 11th District also approved of Jordan's performance. In 1968, Jordan ran unopposed for a second state senate term and won. New state election rules extended her term from two to four years.

Jordan was now a trusted senator—a liberal who supported issues that were in the best interest of the people of Texas. She served on more than ten senate committees, covering issues such as labor and management relations, education, finance, environmental matters, youth affairs, and unemployment benefits for state employees.

Despite Jordan's full schedule, her interest in civil rights law did not wane. The consistent protest of civil rights leaders across the country convinced most politicians that federal laws were necessary to secure equal rights for black people. President Johnson's Great Society campaign inspired Jordan to work even harder for social progress at the state level. But in April 1968, Jordan and other black people across the nation feared that the Civil Rights movement had come to an end.

Dr. Martin Luther King Jr. was assassinated at a motel in Memphis, Tennessee, on April 4. Jordan was at a state fair in San Antonio, Texas, when she heard the tragic news. She was overcome with grief. Several months later, President Johnson announced that he would not run for a

Jordan as a Texas state senator

second term. These events jeopardized the future of civil rights and the Great Society campaign.

Jordan traveled to Chicago in the summer to attend the Democratic National Convention. Delegates from 50 states and all U.S. territories came to the convention to select candidates to run for president and vice president in the upcoming

November election. Since President Johnson refused to run for office, the Democratic Party selected a new presidential candidate. Jordan served as a state delegate for Texas and voted to nominate Hubert H. Humphrey, Johnson's vice president, as the Democratic candidate.

Jordan continued to work for laws that promoted social change throughout the final two years of her second term. She wrote bills guaranteeing housing loans for poor families, equal rights for women, unemployment benefits for people out of work, and job training for the disabled. But after six years in the state senate, Jordan set her sights on a more ambitious goal—a seat in the U.S. House of Representatives in Washington, D.C.

Jordan planned her congressional campaign carefully. She focused on her legislative record and held a major fundraiser at the Rice Hotel in Houston in October 1971. Friends, family, business people, educators, political allies, and grassroots activists attended the gala affair.

> **"Barbara Jordan proved to us that black is beautiful before we knew what that meant."**
>
> —President Lyndon B. Johnson

President Johnson also appeared and pledged his support in a moving speech. "Barbara Jordan proved to us that black is beautiful before we knew what that meant," the president told the crowd of well-wishers. "Wherever she goes, she is going to be at the top."

The fundraiser was a tremendous success. However, Jordan's father was too ill to join her at the festivities. Benjamin Jordan's heart was failing. He no longer worked at the warehouse or preached at his community church. Jordan and

Jordan embraces LBJ at her fundraiser at the Rice Hotel in October 1971.

her family sensed that his death was only a matter of time, but the campaign for the congressional seat moved forward. If Jordan achieved her goal, she would be the first black woman from Texas to be elected to the U.S. House of Representatives—an honor her father would cherish until his last day.

In December, Jordan announced her candidacy and ran a six-month primary race against Curtis Graves, a black Democrat who won a seat in the Texas House of Representatives along with Jordan in 1966. Jordan traveled throughout Harris County reminding voters of her commitment to the people of Texas. On May 6, 1972, she defeated Graves in the Democratic primary, pulling in 80 percent of the vote.

Jordan was unstoppable. She remained a hometown favorite in Houston's Fifth Ward and appealed to the many working-class and liberal voters who believed she worked to protect the rights of the disadvantaged. If Jordan won in the November election against Republican Paul Merit, she would make history.

In April 1972, the Texas State Senate elected Jordan president pro tempore. The president pro tempore post, given to a member of the state senate, was a Texas political tradition. At some point during the term, when the governor and lieutenant governor were both out of state, the president pro tempore would serve as state governor for one day.

Jordan's opportunity came on June 10, 1972. While Governor Preston Smith and Lieutenant Governor Ben Barnes attended to business outside the state, the state senate named Jordan Governor for a Day, giving her the honor to serve as the state's highest official. Jordan was the first black woman to earn the title. Her swearing-in ceremony took place in the Texas Senate chamber, a room filled with political colleagues, family, and friends. The choir from Good Hope Missionary Baptist church, Jordan's childhood spiritual home, performed at the end of the ceremony.

Jordan's father lived to see his daughter sworn-in as governor. Before the festivities were over, however, he suffered a heart attack and died the next morning at a hospital in Austin. Jordan's only comfort was the pride she saw in her father's eyes when she won the Democratic congressional primary in May.

Jordan was elected to the U.S. House of Representatives in another landslide victory in November 1972. Her life would never be the same.

JORDAN IN THE HOUSE

On the same day that Jordan was elected to the House of Representatives, President Richard

*Jordan is sworn in as Governor
for a Day on June 10, 1972.*

Nixon won his reelection campaign. In the months
to come, details of the Watergate scandal would
keep him in the nation's spotlight. In the meantime, Jordan made plans to move to Washington,
D.C., to join other new Congress members at the
opening of the 93rd Congress on January 3, 1973.

Jordan's political future was bright. Her success as a state legislator made her introduction to Congress a bit easier, but she still needed to learn the ropes. Several weeks after the November election, Jordan enrolled in the John F. Kennedy Institute of Politics at Harvard University in Boston to learn more about how politicians work in Congress. She spent most of her time taking notes and thinking hard about the committee assignments she hoped to land in Congress.

Jordan hoped to work on the House Judiciary Committee. It was unusual for a freshman member of Congress to win such an influential assignment. Nevertheless, Jordan wrote to the now-retired President Johnson and asked his advice on the best committee to choose, expressing her desire to work on the Judiciary Committee. The president called Jordan at the Institute and told her he had contacted a few allies to help get her the judiciary assignment. Jordan thanked the president for his assistance. When she completed her studies at the Institute and arrived in the nation's capital, she learned that a seat on the Judiciary Committee had been set aside for her. Jordan was now ready to roll up her sleeves and get down to business with the other 434 members of the House.

Unfortunately, President Johnson did not live to see his political protégée make her mark in Congress. On January 22, 1973, Johnson died of a

As a new member of the House of Representatives in January 1973, Jordan sits with five other women in the House. From left to right are Rep. Martha W. Griffiths (MI), Rep. Shirley Chisholm (NY), Rep. Elizabeth Holtzman (NY), Rep. Jordan (TX), Rep. Yvonne Braithwaite Burke (CA), and Rep. Bella Abzug (NY).

heart attack at his ranch in Texas. In tribute to the former president, Jordan read a touching personal statement on the floor of the House. "The death of Lyndon Johnson diminishes the lives of every American involved with mankind," Jordan said. "Lyndon Johnson was my political mentor and my friend. I loved him and I shall miss him."

Several months later, Jordan's own health was threatened, and she was not able to appear in Congress to cast her vote against Gerald Ford, President Nixon's vice presidential nominee. She was taken to the hospital instead for a week of medical tests. Jordan reportedly suffered from numbness in the arms and legs, but the medical tests did not reveal the cause of her ailment.

Jordan returned to work and kept her health concerns to herself. She began to research and write new civil rights requirements for the Omnibus Crime Control and Safe Streets Act. This four-year-old law provided federal money for state and local governments to develop community-based programs to decrease crime rates and improve living conditions in jails. Jordan wanted the law to include civil rights requirements to make sure the community-based programs did not discriminate on the basis of "race, color, national origin, or sex."

The civil rights requirements became known as the Jordan Amendment. The amendment was approved by Congress and the Judiciary Committee. Jordan had won her first legislative victory in Congress.

A month after the Watergate hearings, Jordan was one of the most popular black political leaders in the country. Her historic legal argument persuaded many Americans to believe the president would be tried in a court of law, but this never happened.

On August 9, 1974, Richard Milhous Nixon submitted his resignation to Congress. Vice President Gerald Ford was immediately sworn in as the 38th president of the United States. One month later, President Ford granted Nixon a pardon for all federal crimes the former president may have committed during his administration.

Jordan was out of the country when she heard the news about the presidential pardon. "What the hell are you talking about?" she replied when a news reporter called her in China to ask for her comment. Jordan and several other members of Congress were visiting China for an important

"The country was definitely short-changed."

fact-finding trip. The presidential pardon seemed like an insult. "I felt cheated," Jordan said in her autobiography. "Something at least could have been resolved with the finality of a court decision, but now everything is wiped out ... the country was definitely short-changed."

Jordan flew back to the states to run for a second congressional term. In November 1974, she won more than 80 percent of the vote in her congressional district. Jordan returned to the House and continued her work for civil rights. She wrote additional laws to guarantee the proper enforcement of the Jordan Amendment in the Omnibus Crime Control and Safe Streets Act and worked to extend the legal protections of the Voting Rights Act of 1965 to Latinos, American Indians, Alaskan Natives, and Asian Americans.

Jordan supported civil rights for people of color, but she did not embrace the growing Black Power movement that flourished in poor black communities in the northern and western United States. The Black Panthers, a group of young black political activists, were influential in the movement and encouraged black Americans to honor their African ancestry. The Panthers also demanded that the federal government pay black Americans for the free labor of their enslaved ancestors, and they urged black people to defend themselves against police violence. Unlike traditional civil rights leaders who encouraged blacks to participate in America's mainstream political, economic, and social system, the Black Panthers urged blacks to patronize businesses in the black community, form a separate political party, and support all-black educational institutions.

The media often photographed Black Panther members holding firearms, and several of the group's members clashed with the police. As a result, many police authorities, political officials, and some civil rights leaders viewed the Panthers as a militant and radical protest group. Jordan carefully distanced herself from the more aggressive message of the Black Power movement. "All blacks are militant in their guts," Jordan said in a 1970 interview with the *Houston Post*. "But militancy is expressed in various ways. Some do it quite overtly, while others try to work their way through the system, trying to bring about changes in race and human relations. That's the way I like to work. Disruptive or divisive kinds of behavior is no help."

Many people viewed the Black Panthers, shown here in New York City in July 1968, as a militant protest group. Jordan distanced herself from the more aggressive elements of the movement.

Jordan's political and legal experience strengthened her belief that only political equality would guarantee black people economic and social justice. Jordan believed the same rule applied to women's rights.

In 1974, the Equal Rights Amendment (ERA), a bill that proposed to guarantee all Americans the "equality of rights under law, regardless of their gender," was approaching its deadline for ratification by state legislatures. Congress approved the proposal two years earlier, but ratification by three-fourths (38) of the states is required in order for a proposed amendment to become part of the Constitution. Critics of the ERA argued that the Constitution already provides women with equal protection under the law. Supporters, however, declared that despite the Constitution's legal protections, women often do not receive equal treatment in federal or state courts.

Jordan joined other members of Congress to support legislation that would extend the ERA's approval deadline from 1979 to 1986 so that the issue could be debated longer. Jordan supported the legal theory behind the bill, but in her personal life she believed equal rights for women came from changes in attitude, not changes in law. "She [Jordan] assumed that any woman who made the same single-minded decision to give career [the] first priori-ty that she had, could excel," wrote Shelby Hearon, coauthor of Jordan's autobiogra-phy. "For this reason, women's progress seemed more a matter of attitude to her."

"Women's progress seemed more a matter of attitude to her."
—Shelby Hearon

However, Jordan the politician recognized the need for women's rights around the world. On November 10, 1975, a year after she voted to extend the ERA deadline, Jordan spoke out for equal rights and women's self-esteem in a speech at the Lyndon B. Johnson School of Public Affairs in Austin, Texas. Jordan gave the speech as part of the United Nation's International Women's Year.

"I don't care which country you would like to view—Britain, Sweden, Finland, Denmark—the problem is the same. The women at the bottom, men at the top," Jordan said. "So what are we going to do about it. . . . How are we going to reverse the trend that has women at the bottom of whatever profession we talk about. . . . It's going to take long, hard, slow, tedious work. And we begin with ourselves. We begin with our own self-concept."

Jordan's strong views about a healthy self-esteem mirrored changes in her own life. Jordan had shed close to 60 pounds (27 kg) from her full-figured frame. She realized that her physical appearance was now an important part of her public appeal, and she had grown tired of press reports that described her as "hulking" and "massive." Jordan could no longer ignore the connection between her image and her political popularity and success. She was one of the most respected black women in politics, and she was determined to look the part.

A KEYNOTE SUCCESS

On July 2, 1976, Jordan stepped onto the speaking podium at the Democratic National Convention at Madison Square Garden in New York City. Convention organizers had asked Jordan and Senator John Glenn, a Democrat from Ohio, each to deliver a rousing keynote speech before a large crowd of Democratic state delegates and 75 million television viewers.

The delegates packed the Garden to cast their vote for the Democratic presidential ticket in the November election. Jimmy Carter, the soft-spoken governor of Georgia, and Walter Mondale, a senator from Minnesota, were favored as the political team for the White House. The Democrats hoped the party would win an overwhelming victory in the elections. The Republicans, led by President

Jordan acknowledges the cheering audience after delivering her keynote address in 1976.

Ford, struggled to regain the public's trust after Watergate.

Democratic leaders assumed Senator Glenn's speech would be the highlight of the convention. Glenn, a former astronaut, became the first American to orbit the earth in 1962. His popularity was unquestionable. But his long-winded speech fell on deaf ears. The delegates talked among themselves and paid little attention to the national hero. Jordan, on the other hand, turned the convention's nervous rattlings into respectful silence.

Her trim figure and signature forthright style captured the delegates' attention. Jordan's stomach quivered when she looked into the bright television cameras, but she calmly waved at her audience and flashed a big smile. Once again, she delivered a speech that would long be remembered.

> There is something different about tonight. There is something special about tonight. What is different? What is special? I, Barbara Jordan, am a keynote speaker.
>
> A lot of years passed since 1832, [the year of the first Democratic National Convention], and during that time it would have been most unusual for any national political party to ask that a Barbara Jordan deliver a keynote address . . . but tonight here I am. And I feel, notwithstanding the past, that my presence here is one additional bit of evidence that the American Dream need not forever be deferred.

The audience punctuated each of Jordan's points with wild cheers. She concluded her remarks with these words:

> Now, I began this speech by commenting to you on the uniqueness of a Barbara Jordan making the keynote address. Well, I am going to close my speech by quoting a

Republican President, and I ask that as you listen to these words of Abraham Lincoln you relate them to the concept of a national community in which every last one of us participates: "As I would not be a slave, so I would not be a master. This expresses my idea of democracy. Whatever differs from this, to the extent of the difference, is no democracy."

A deafening round of applause swept through the convention hall. The delegates shouted "We want Barbara" and waved their state banners in the air. Democratic party leaders swelled with pride. Jordan's steadfast belief in democratic government and her devotion to social justice reflected the moral values her party espoused. Once again, Jordan, now 40, was catapulted onto the national stage. Her political colleagues considered her to be a strong candidate for the vice-presidential nomination.

The next morning, news of Jordan's speech made the front page of every major newspaper across the country. The *Houston Post* called Jordan "a national superstar." The *New York Times* chronicled Jordan's rise in politics and called her latest triumph "a classic American success story." The entire nation wondered what would be the next step for this dynamic politician. Barbara Jordan would surprise them all.

CHAPTER FIVE

GOOD-BYE CONGRESS

President-elect Jimmy Carter and Vice President-elect Walter Mondale won the 1976 election, and Jordan was elected to her third congressional term in the 95th Congress. Carter asked Jordan to serve in his administration and met with her in private after the Democratic National Convention. The two politicians also spoke by telephone. The vice presidency was no longer an option for Jordan, but she hoped she could serve the country as attorney general. Carter and Jordan discussed the position and her qualifications, but when the negotiations ended, Jordan returned to Congress.

Jordan was no longer content writing congressional legislation or working with her political allies to protect the interests of the 18th congressional district. Jordan wanted to use her status as a well-known public figure to speak out on important social and economic issues, such as health care, unemployment, and the need for a politically active public. Jordan felt confined by the limitations of her political office. She wanted a new challenge.

In June 1977, Jordan became the first black woman to deliver a commencement address at Harvard University. She also received a honorary degree from the university. Other honorary degree recipients at the ceremony included black opera singer Marian Anderson, novelist Eudora Welty, financier Albert Gordon, botanist Paul Mangelsdorf, lawyer-historian Paul Freund, and Oxford scholar Sir Richard Southern. When Jordan received the letter informing her of the honorary degree, she felt honored. And when a second letter came asking her to deliver the commencement address, Jordan was "very pleased."

The audience responded with awe and genuine warmth when Jordan delivered her address. For Jordan, the event was special for personal reasons. "Sometimes I just stare in the mirror and look at myself and say, 'Barbara, by golly, you've done okay. It wasn't easy, but you've done okay'," Jordan said to friends and family members after her speech. She recalled when

"Sometimes I just stare in the mirror and look at myself and say, 'Barbara, by golly, you've done okay.'"

her college debate coach Dr. Tom Freeman advised her not to set her sights on Harvard. "[He] told me I'd never get into Harvard, not to apply. But here I am. I did get in," Jordan said proudly. "Right now here I am. I'm in!"

For the remainder of her congressional term, Jordan quietly planned her transition to private

Barbara Jordan (right) greets acclaimed opera singer Marian Anderson (left) before both received honorary degrees from Harvard University on June 16, 1977. Both these women had broken down racial barriers during their celebrated careers.

life. She also began to notice subtle changes in her health. Jordan managed to lose an additional 30 pounds (14 kg), but despite her recent weight loss, her body seemed to be deteriorating before her eyes. A year earlier, she had struggled to balance her weight on a weak knee as she walked up to the speaker's podium at the Democratic National Convention. Jordan continued to suffer in silence and shared her plans for a new career with no one but very close friends and family.

On December 10, 1977, Jordan announced her plans to retire from political life and return to Texas. She would not run for a fourth congressional term and, contrary to rumor, she had no plans to campaign for the presidency or any other executive office. Jordan's colleagues in Washington, D.C., and Texas were surprised. No one expected Jordan to withdraw from politics. After six years of service on Capitol Hill, however, Jordan was ready to say good-bye.

LIFE AFTER CONGRESS

She returned home to Texas in 1978 and accepted a teaching position at the LBJ School of Public Affairs at the University of Texas at Austin. Jordan's two classes—policy development and political values and ethics—were so popular, students were selected for the courses through a lottery.

Jordan announces her retirement from the House of Representatives on December 10, 1977.

Professor Jordan soon earned a new reputation as a tough teacher who gave her students long reading assignments and expected them to debate issues intelligently. She also helped to counsel students and recruit people of color to the campus. To ensure that her years of political contributions would help educate students, Jordan donated all of her public and professional papers and speeches, as well as the furniture from her congressional and legal offices, to Texas Southern University, her alma mater.

Jordan's new teaching role gave her the free time to enjoy her hobbies—singing, playing guitar, and reading mysteries and biographies. She also settled permanently into a new home with long-time friend Nancy Earl. Eventually, the cause of Jordan's health concerns was discovered. She was diagnosed with multiple sclerosis—a disorder that attacks the body's nervous system. Jordan's return to private life helped her to manage her new physical disability.

Retirement agreed with Jordan. She loved teaching and often traveled to make speeches about important social issues. "I enjoy teaching my students," Jordan said. "I have the opportunity to impact the next generation of public officials in what I do, and that pleases me."

Jordan no longer lived in the national spotlight, but her reputation as a champion of liberal causes was not forgotten. Television producer Norman Lear called Jordan in 1980 to help create People for the American Way, a nonpartisan organization dedicated to protecting and promoting the constitutional rights of all Americans. Jordan did not hesitate to lend her support. She became a member of the organization's Board of Directors and worked closely with its staff to raise money and produce television commercials. "All of us had such reverence for her," remembers Barbara Handman, vice president and director of the organization's New York office. "I don't know anyone else who would need to commit their life to the constitution, except maybe a Supreme Court judge. It was her guide for everything."

In 1980, Jordan (left) became a founding member of People for the American Way. Legendary black singer Lena Horne (right) also supported the organization.

Seven years later, Jordan returned to Washington, D.C., to speak out against the nomination of Judge Robert H. Bork to the Supreme Court. Jordan recalled Bork's controversial move to fire Archibald Cox, the special prosecutor in the Watergate scandal. She feared Bork would try to eliminate important laws for citizens' rights. President Ronald Reagan, a conservative Republican elected in 1980, nominated Bork to the Court. Several organizations, including People for the American Way, launched a public-awareness campaign to prevent Bork from serving on the Court.

Jordan firmly believed that Bork was not a suitable Court candidate, and she testified before the Senate Judiciary Committee to prove her point. In her testimony before the Committee, Jordan recalled the Supreme Court mandate that prompted Harrison County to redraw the boundaries of the 11th Senatorial District in Texas and enabled her to make a successful run for the state legislature and begin a career in politics in the 1960s. The Court upheld the principle that all votes should be valued equally—regardless of the race of the voter. This principle is sometimes referred to as "one person, one vote."

"Do you know what Judge Bork says about those [court cases] on reapportionment? He has disagreed with the principle of one person, one vote many times," Jordan urgently explained. She added that Bork once called the principle a "straight jacket" that had no "theoretical basis" in the law. "Maybe there is no theoretical basis for one person, one vote, but I will tell you this much. There is a common sense, natural, rational basis for all votes counting equally."

> **"There is a common sense, natural, rational basis for all votes counting equally."**

Jordan continued, "My opposition to this nomination is really a result of my living 51 years as a black American living in the South and determined to be heard by the majority community. . . . When you experience the frustration of being a minority and watching the foreclosure of your last [legal] appeal, and then suddenly you are rescued by the Supreme Court of the United States, Mr. Chairman, that is tantamount to being born again."

The Senate did not confirm Judge Bork's nomination, and Jordan and other liberals breathed a sigh of relief. The Democrats once again called on Jordan to be a keynote speaker at the Democratic National Convention in 1988. Jordan, now bound to a wheelchair, accepted the invitation and supported the nomination of Lloyd Bentsen, a Texas senator, for vice president. The delegates welcomed Jordan's return to the speaker's podium and cheered her remarks on party

Jordan testifies against the nomination of Robert Bork to the Supreme Court.

unity and sound political judgment. Democratic presidential candidate Michael Dukakis, a governor from Massachusetts, and Bentsen lost the November election to George Bush and his running mate, Dan Quayle. The conservative Republican win convinced Jordan that the era of liberal politics that flourished during the 1960s and 1970s was being replaced by a period of conservative economic and social reform in the states and military confrontations abroad. The nation's political tide was shifting. Jordan now hoped she could continue to defend the legal liberties she worked so hard to guarantee for others.

NEAR TRAGEDY

Unfortunately, several weeks after the Democratic convention, Jordan made national news in a dreadful way. She almost lost her life in a mysterious swimming accident. Jordan was rushed to a hospital in Austin in August 1988 after she was found unconscious in her home swimming pool. She recovered quickly, but she never publicly revealed the cause of the accident. Press reports noted that Jordan's doctors believed she was lucky to survive the accident without serious brain damage. Her recuperation was a miracle.

People for the American Way honored Jordan in a gala event in New York City on November 18, 1988. Jordan traveled to New York to receive the organization's Spirit of Liberty Award for her political and professional commitment to the principles of the constitution. Norman Lear hosted the black-tie event, and singer Dionne Warwick and comedian Billy Crystal entertained the audience.

Jordan used the prestigious event to voice her concerns about the nation's conservative political climate and the dismantling of important civil rights laws.

"Liberty is one of those defining attributes of the American people and the American nation. If it is to last as a bright and untarnished symbol, the people of America must work to preserve and protect it," Jordan said in her award acceptance speech. "Ever the guardian of liberty, we must be eternal in our vigilance and unyielding in our defense."

Jordan continued, "All of us as a nation bear the exquisite burden of assuring that all our citizens—not only those with the best handlers, the snappiest sound bites, the cleverest lawyers, and the largest bank accounts—can claim liberty as their own. For liberty becomes endangered when its sister virtue, equality, is threatened."

In 1992, Jordan was hopeful that Bill Clinton, governor of Arkansas and a Democratic presidential candidate, could lead the country to a political middle ground that would protect civil liberties. Ever the faithful southern Democrat, Jordan

"We are one, we Americans, and we reject any intruder who seeks to divide us by race or class."

Jordan waves to the crowd after delivering her third and final keynote address at the 1992 Democratic National Convention.

delivered what would become her final Democratic National Convention speech.

"We are one, we Americans, and we reject any intruder who seeks to divide us by race or class. We seek to unite people, not to divide them, and we reject both white racism and black racism," Jordan said in her speech. "This party will not tolerate bigotry under any guise."

Jordan's remark regarding "black racism" was not well received by some black leaders who argued that the term was politically unwise. Clinton campaigned for the Democratic nomination against Reverend Jesse Jackson, a black minister and civil rights activist who proposed a more liberal political platform than his opponent. Some black leaders were concerned Jordan's speech was a sign she had aligned herself with the Democrats' traditional politics and white-male leadership.

Jordan returned home to Texas, but the controversy surrounding her speech left some black leaders with questions about her view of the political debates raised during the convention. Jordan's political insight and moral authority still commanded respect, but the nation's landscape had become more complex, and other black leaders also captured the public's attention. Now approaching her sixth decade of life, Jordan was certain of one truth. The quest for equality for all Americans was far from over.

CHAPTER SIX

TWILIGHT

President Bill Clinton appointed Jordan to head a new Immigration Reform Commission in 1993. This eight-member commission, made up of Democrats, Republicans, and private citizens, was responsible for writing recommendations on how the federal government could improve or change the nation's immigration laws. Jordan quickly moved to start the commission's work.

Immigration has become a hotly debated political issue. Scores of immigrants, mostly from Mexico, flee to the United States from their native homelands every year to find jobs to support their families. Some immigrants who have not obtained the proper immigration documents (such as a green card or social security card) work illegally in the United States without paying taxes. Meanwhile, legally documented workers often struggle to make ends meet in low paying jobs.

Critics of the nation's immigration laws insist that the government allows too many immigrants to enter the country, taking jobs away from American workers. Others argue that undocumented workers pay no taxes and therefore are not entitled to government benefits, such as public schooling and health care. Advocates for immigration rights say political leaders should work to improve the law enforcement agencies that patrol our nation's borders and the federal agencies that serve immigrants. These advocates remind us of the vital role immigration has played in the history and tradition of the United States.

For the past several years, the debate has been fierce. In 1994, the state legislature and people of California considered the merits of Proposition 187, a proposal to prevent the state from giving health, welfare, or educational benefits to illegal immigrants or their children. Jordan opposed Proposition 187, but many of the Immigration Reform Commission's members supported the proposal. Jordan was determined to put the political debate aside and work with all the members to write fair recommendations.

The Commission wrote a full-length immigration report and a list of recommendations for President Clinton's approval. Jordan met with Clinton aides at the White House in September 1994 to discuss the report and later held a press conference at the National Press Club to present the recommendations to the press. The Commission advised the president to create a national registry of all workers in the nation to track social security numbers and locate undocumented immigrant workers. The national registry proposal raised many eyebrows. Critics immediately charged that the registry would be a violation of privacy rights.

> **"If we are to preserve our immigration tradition . . . we've got to have the strength to say 'No' to the people who are not supposed to get in."**

"We disagree with those who label our efforts to control immigration as anti-immigrant," Jordan said at the news conference, adding she loathed immigrant bashing. "If we are to preserve our immigration tradition . . . we've got to have the strength to say 'No' to the people who are not supposed to get in."

Jordan listened to the critics, but she refused to discount the Commission's investigation. Rumors soon spread that President Clinton would not support the Commission's report, but Jordan would not be moved. She promised the Commission would renew its investigation if its recommendations were not effective. Jordan waited patiently for the president's response.

In January 1996, President Clinton publicly announced his support for the Commission and its recommendations in his State of the Union Address. The Commission also received approval to remain active for three more years. But Jordan's leadership on the Commission would be her final duty in public service.

PASSING OF A HERO

On January 17, 1996, Barbara Charline Jordan died from viral pneumonia and complications of leukemia in Austin, Texas. She was 59 years old. More than 2,000 mourners, including the president, attended the funeral at the Good Hope Missionary Baptist Church, Jordan's childhood church. Jordan's family, friends, and political colleagues came to pay their respects. Those attending included Ann Richards, the former governor of Texas. Five years earlier, Richards appointed Jordan to be the Special Counsel for Ethics—a personal adviser to the governor. Andrew Young, the former mayor of Atlanta, Dr. Thomas Freeman, Jordan's former debate coach, and actress Cicley Tyson also attended the funeral.

Jordan's body lay in an oak casket, draped with the American flag and surrounded by bouquets of flowers. "With the poetry of her words and the power of her voice, Barbara always stirred our national conscience," said President

A large crowd gathers to pay respects to Barbara Jordan at her funeral on January 20, 1996.

Clinton in a speech at the funeral. "She did it as a legislator, a member of Congress, a teacher, a citizen. Perhaps more than anything else in the last few years, for those of us who had the privilege of being around her, she did it with the incredible grace and good humor and dignity with which she bore her physical misfortunes. No matter what, there was always the dignity."

> **"With the poetry of her words and the power of her voice, Barbara always stirred our national conscience."**
> —President Bill Clinton

In the last years of her life, Jordan received numerous awards and honors. She was given the Presidential Medal of Freedom, one of the nation's highest honors, from President Clinton in 1994. (The medal was placed on Jordan's lapel for her funeral.) She was also named to the Lyndon Johnson chair in National Policy at the LBJ School of Public Affairs during the same year. In 1984, she was named Outstanding Woman by the American Association of University Women and the Best Living Orator by the International Platform Association.

Jordan received more than 25 honorary degrees from universities across the country, including Texas Southern University, Boston University, Princeton University, Howard University, and Notre Dame University. In addition to her autobiography, Jordan also wrote several legal books and articles.

Jordan dedicated much of her free time to young people. She frequently visited public elementary and high schools to encourage students to stay in school and to register to vote at age 18.

"She loved young people and enjoyed talking to them," recalls Barbara Handman of People for the American Way. "She tried to convince them of her [legal] arguments and her dedication to the values of the constitution."

Jordan remained socially active, despite her physical disability. "She didn't give up," says

Clinton presents Jordan with the Presidential Medal of Freedom in 1994.

Handman, remembering a time in 1988 when a wheelchair ramp was built in the middle of the night to help Jordan gain access to a friend's house for dinner in New York. "You went through these difficulties with her when you were committed to Barbara."

In her last will and testament, Jordan reiterated her gift of her public and professional papers and speeches to the Barbara Jordan Archives at Texas Southern University, her alma mater. She also gave 15 percent of her taxable estate to People for the American Way, Inc., Helping Our Brothers Out, Inc., and AIDS Services of Austin, Inc.—three charitable groups.

In tribute to Jordan, the University of Texas at Austin now sponsors the Annual Barbara Jordan Historical Essay Competition, formerly called the Annual African-American Historical Essay Competition. Jordan served as the official spokesperson for the first competition shortly before her death.

High school students who enter the contest are required to "research and write history about their communities throughout Texas." Twenty-four finalists are selected to represent their respective regions at the state competition. The three state winners each receive a scholarship ranging from $1,000 to $2,500. All of the 24 essays are archived at the university's Center for American History. Each finalist also receives a medallion designed from a head bust of Jordan.

Barbara Charline Jordan made history several times in her life through sheer determination and the power of her mind. She became a highly respected and admired politician and legal expert, battling racism, sexism, and poverty along the

Throughout her career, Jordan dedicated much of her free time to young people.

way. Jordan used her scholarly education and experience to improve the lives of the less fortunate, and she worked diligently to defend the rights of the loyal Texas voters who believed in her. Jordan never sought fame, but she became a national figure when she dared to speak the truth. Jordan never shied away from criticism and refused to compromise her personal convictions, no matter how controversial the debate.

Jordan became the person her grandfather Patten had hoped. Perhaps this was her most important achievement and her greatest source of pride at the end of her life.

"It is really one of the most incredible facts of my life . . . people come up to me and quote things I have said, things I don't remember saying," Jordan told a newspaper reporter in 1992. "I don't understand it. I don't need to. There are so many people in public life who are not remembered."

Fortunately for all Americans, Barbara Charline Jordan and her many achievements will be honored for years to come.

CHRONOLOGY

1936	Barbara Charline Jordan born February 21, Houston, Texas.
1952	Graduates from Phyllis Wheatley High School.
1956	Graduates from Texas Southern University, Magna Cum Laude.
1959	Graduates from Boston University Law School.
1961	Teaches at Tuskegee Institute and opens law practice in downtown Houston.
1962	Runs for Texas House of Representatives.
1964	Runs for Texas House of Representatives.
1965	Serves as an administrative assistant for Judge William Elliot in Harris County.
1966	Wins election to Texas House of Representatives, first black state senator since 1883, closes law office in downtown Houston.
1972	Serves as Governor for the Day on June 10. Wins November election to serve in the U.S. House of Representatives, becoming the first black woman to represent Texas.
1973	Appointed to House Judiciary Committee.

1974	Delivers speech recommending impeachment of President Richard M. Nixon. Reelected to U.S. House of Representatives; serves as a member of a fact-finding mission to China.
1976	Becomes the first black person to deliver a keynote speech at the Democratic National Convention. Reelected to third term in the U.S. House of Representatives.
1978	Retires from Congress.
1979	Accepts a professorship at the Lyndon B. Johnson School of Public Affairs, University of Texas at Austin.
1980	Becomes a founding member of People for the American Way.
1987	Testifies before Senate Judiciary Committee against the Supreme Court nomination of judge Robert Bork.
1988	Delivers a keynote speech at the Democratic National Convention in July. Found unconscious in her swimming pool in Austin, Texas, and taken to a nearby hospital in August. Recuperation successful, but cause of accident is not disclosed. Accepts the Spirit of Liberty Award from People for the American Way in November.
1992	Delivers her final Democratic National Convention speech.
1993	Appointed to chair the U.S. Commission on Immigration Reform.
1994	Awarded Medal of Freedom from President Bill Clinton.
1996	Dies from viral pneumonia and complications of leukemia on January 17 in Austin, Texas.

BOOKS

The definitive text of Barbara Jordan's life is *Barbara Jordan: A Self-Portrait*, her autobiography (Doubleday, 1979). Jordan coauthored the book with Shelby Hearon, an author of five novels, and a writing instructor at the University of Texas at Austin. It offers Jordan's personal thoughts and recollections in her signature forthright style, and Hearon's objective analysis of Jordan's political rise, her achievements, and their impact on her life as a black woman. *Barbara Jordan: Politician*, by Rose Blue and Corinne Naden (Chelsea House Publishers, 1992) is an ideal text for middle school and teenage readers. The book is informative, entertaining, and it emphasizes Jordan's historical role in American politics. *African American Women in Congress: Forming and Transforming Society*, by LaVerne McCain Gill (Rutgers University Press, 1997), is collection of 15 biographies of the nation's prominent African American congresswomen. McCain Gill, a radio and television journalist, drew much of her research from "The Talented Ten: African American Women in the 103rd Congress," a public radio program she created in 1994. The book, targeted to adult readers, provides an objective examination of the lives and contributions of black women in Congress and their impact on U.S. public policy and the political attitudes of American voters.

PERIODICALS

Magazine articles about Jordan's life, political attitudes, and the bequeath of her estate at the time of her death include "Barbara Jordan," 1993 Current Biography Yearbook, H. W. Company, New York; "Fiercely Private Barbara Jordan Goes Public with Immigration Reform," *Knight Ridder/Tribune News Service*, October 1994; "Barbara Jordan: A Woman of Her Words," *Washington Post*, January 18, 1996; "Barbara Jordan Wills Her Estate to Sisters, Friend, and Mother," *Jet*, February 12, 1996; "Major Barbara," *Texas Monthly*, March 1996.

OTHER SOURCES

Barbara Jordan's public and private speeches excerpted and reprinted with the permission of the Barbara Jordan Archives at Texas Southern University.

Barbara Jordan's testimony before the U.S. Senate Committee on the Judiciary, September 21, 1987, regarding the nomination of judge Robert Bork, courtesy of People for the American Way.

Barbara Jordan's speech, "Is Our Stewardship of Liberty Flagging," for the acceptance of the Spirit of Liberty Award on November 17, 1988, courtesy of People for the American Way.

Telephone interview with Barbara Handman, vice president and director of People for the American Way, New York, held on July 25, 1997.

FOR MORE INFORMATION

BOOKS FOR YOUNGER READERS

Blue, Rose, and Corinne Naden. *Barbara Jordan: Politician.* New York: Chelsea House, 1992.

Fireside, Bryna J. *Is there a Woman in the House—or Senate?* Morton Grove, IL: A. Whitman & Co., 1994.

Jeffrey, Laura S. *Barbara Jordan: Congresswoman, Lawyer, Educator.* Springfield, NJ: Enslow, 1997.

Lindop, Laurie. *Political Leaders.* New York : Twenty-First Century Books, 1996.

Morin, Isobel V. *Women of the United States Congress.* Minneapolis: Oliver Press, 1994.

Pollack, Jill S. *Women on the Hill: The History of Women in Congress.* Danbury, CT: Franklin Watts, 1996.

Winegarten, Ruthe. *Brave Black Women: From Slavery to the Space Shuttle.* Austin: University of Texas Press, 1997

BOOKS FOR OLDER READERS

Gill, LaVerne McCain. *African American Women in Congress: Forming and Transforming Society.*

New Brunswick, NJ: Rutgers University Press, 1997.

Jordan, Barbara, and Shelby Hearon. *Barbara Jordan: A Self-Portrait*. New York: Doubleday, 1979.

INTERNET RESOURCES

Barbara Jordan
http://www.rice.edu/armadillo/Texas/jordan.html
This excellent Barbara Jordan page is a collection of news stories, essays, tributes, and other material related to Barbara Jordan and her work.

Barbara Jordan Page
http://www.lib.utexas.edu/Libs/PAL/jordan/jordan.html
Information about Barbara Jordan including a biography and transcripts of speeches. Maintained by the Edie and Lew Wasserman Public Affairs Library at the University of Texas, Austin, TX.

The First and Only
http://www.pbs.org/newshour/bb/remember/jordan_1-17.html
The site contains the transcript of a PBS memorial to Barbara Jordan.

President Bill Clinton's Speech Delivered at Barbara Jordan's Funeral
http://www2.whitehouse.gov/WH/New/other/bjordan.html
This page on the White House Web site contains the text of President Clinton's speech delivered at Barbara Jordan's funeral.

U.S. House of Representatives
http://www.house.gov/
Barbara Jordan served in the U.S. House of Representatives from 1973 to 1978. This is the official site of the U.S. House of Representatives.

INDEX

Page numbers in *italics* indicate illustrations.

ABOUT THE AUTHOR

Lisa Renee Rhodes is a journalist and writer of literature for children and young adults. Ms. Rhodes is a graduate of Bernard M. Baruch College, City University of New York, and the Columbia Graduate School of Journalism.

J
B
Jordan
R

Rhodes, Lisa Renee.

Barbara Jordan.

BAKER & TAYLOR